The Bordon Light Railway

Peter A. Harding

M7 class 0-4-4T No.30110 with a pull-and-push two carriage set at Bordon Station on September 14th 1957.
S.C.Nash

Published by

Peter A. Harding

"Mossgiel", Bagshot Road, Knaphill,
Woking, Surrey GU21 2SG.

ISBN 978 0 9552403 5 5
First published 1987. Revised edition 2010.
© Peter A. Harding 2010.
Printed by Binfield Print & Design Ltd.,
Binfield Road, Byfleet Village, Surrey KT14 7PN.

Contents

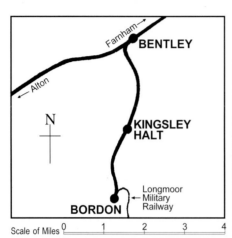

M7 class 0-4-4T No.30028 with a Railway Enthusiasts Club special train at Kingsley Halt on October 15th 1960. Tony Wright

M7 class 0-4-4T No.110 crossing over Sickles Lane at Kingsley with a two carriage pull-and-push set having just left Kingsley Halt for Bordon in the late 1940's. E.C.Griffiths

Introduction

The Bordon Light Railway was authorised under a Light Railway Order in 1902 and was opened on December 11th 1905 to connect the Army Camp at Bordon with the national railway network at Bentley on the main Farnham-Alton line.

Apart from its obvious military usage, the line also served the local community at Bordon and at Kingsley where a small intermediate halt was opened on March 7th 1906.

Although opened as a Light Railway, it was worked in many ways as a normal country branch line and often referred to as the 'Bordon Branch', the line also connected with the Longmoor Military Railway via exchange sidings at Bordon.

During the two world wars the Bordon Light Railway was very heavily used but, by the 1950's passenger traffic had fallen away to such an extent that passenger services were withdrawn from September 1957 although goods services continued until April 1966.

Typical of a variety of rural railways which have now disappeared from the British countryside, the Bordon Light Railway performed a useful function during its existence and is still remembered with much affection in its own locality.

I hope that this booklet will help readers to recapture the charm and atmosphere of this short but interesting country railway.

I dedicate this publication to my late wife Pat who unexpectedly passed away on June 24th 2009 while on holiday in Jersey. Her love, help and support will always be sadly missed. Peter A. Harding

M7 class 0-4-4T No.30027 with pull-and-push two carriage set No.662 leaving Kingsley Halt for Bordon on September 26th 1953.   Denis Cullum

History of the Line

At the turn of the twentieth century, several military camps were built in the vicinity of the London & South Western Railway (LSWR) to accommodate troops on their return from the South African War. Such camps were those at Bulford, Blackdown, Tidworth, Longmoor and Bordon.

The camp at Bordon was built in an agricultural area near the village of Bordon some 4¹/₂ miles to the south of Bentley Station which was situated on the main LSWR line between Farnham and Alton. The camp at Longmoor was about 4¹/₂ miles further south of Bordon.

Because some of the corrugated huts at Longmoor were built on rather soft ground and the two battalions accommodated there, complained, it was decided in 1903 to move not only both battalions but also 68 huts to Bordon.

To save the cost of dismantling and re-erection, the huts were moved bodily on a rather primitive rail link which was quickly constructed and consisted of two parallel railway tracks of 1ft 6ins gauge, the outside rails being 22ft apart. The motive power was by mobile steam winch with the help of a steam ploughing engine and some horses. The huts were moved on 7 pairs of trolleys which were specially made by W.G.Bagnall of Stafford.

Laying the two parallel 1ft 6ins gauge tracks, the outside rails being 22ft apart, to move the army huts from Longmoor Camp to Bordon Camp in 1903. Aldershot Military Historical Trust

One of the army huts being moved to Bordon Camp. Aldershot Military Historical Trust

With all this military activity necessary at Bordon, it seemed that a rail connection with the main LSWR line at Bentley was now urgently required to ease troop movement and facilitate the supply of stores, fodder etc.

As it was, the LSWR with the backing of the War Department had already obtained a Light Railway Order on October 6th 1902 for a 4½ mile long standard gauge single line from Bentley to a terminus just west of Bordon village where it was hoped that the new line would not only serve the military camp but would also serve the local community and farmers alike.

The Light Railway Act of 1896 provided for the avoidance of parliamentary expenses, minimum construction and operating costs plus the availability of financial assistance. It meant, in fact, a rather basic railway with lighter permanent way, sharper curves, steeper gradients, ungated level crossings and minimum signalling with speed restrictions.

LIGHT RAILWAYS ACT 1896.

LONDON & SOUTH WESTERN RAILWAY (BENTLEY & BORDON LIGHT RAILWAY).

[DRAFT]

ORDER

OF THE LIGHT RAILWAY COMMISSIONERS

authorising the construction of a Light Railway in the County of Southampton between Bentley and Bordon.

WHEREAS an application was in pursuance of the Light Railways Act 1896 in November 1901 duly made to the Light Railway Commissioners by the London and South Western Railway Company (hereinafter called "the Company") for an Order to authorise the construction of the light railway hereinafter described NOW we the Light Railway Commissioners being satisfied after local inquiry of the expediency of granting the said application do in pursuance of the said Act and by virtue and in exercise of the powers

A draft copy of the Light Railway Order. Note that the original title was the Bentley & Bordon Light Railway, although the name Bentley was soon dropped.

The LSWR had already made use of the Light Railway Act of 1896 for the building of the nearby Basingstoke and Alton Light Railway in 1901. So, with this experience behind them plus the help of the War Department they were able to acquire the land and construct the new line between Bentley and Bordon without the endless enquiries which accompanied many other similar independent light railways.

The line was built by the LSWR's own staff in just 18 months at a total cost of £30,000. During this time they engaged up to 155 men using 3 locomotives, 4 tip wagons and 3 horses. The three LSWR locomotives used for the construction work were Manning Wardle 0-6-0 saddle tank No.392 formerly called 'Lady Portsmouth', Hawthorn Leslie 0-4-0 saddle tank No.458 'Ironside' and Vulcan Foundry 0-4-0 saddle tank No. 111 'Vulcan'.

Hawthorn Leslie 0-4-0 saddle tank No.458 'Ironside' which was one of the three locomotives used in the construction of the line.
D.L.Bradley Collection

The new light railway was opened from a bay platform at Bentley Station on December 11th 1905 and, possibly because of the War Department involvement, seems to have lacked the usual fanfares and ceremonies that marked most railway openings at this time. The *Farnham Herald* simply covered the event with the following short paragraph in their December 16th 1905 edition:-

The Bentley & Bordon Light Railway was opened to passenger and goods traffic on Monday. Eight trains run from Bentley to Bordon on weekdays and seven from Bordon to Bentley, except on Saturdays, when there are eight. Two trains run each way on Sundays.

Bordon Station soon after opening. One of the narrow gauge trolleys used by the LSWR during construction can be seen on the right of the photograph.   Author's Collection

A slightly later view of the station at Bordon.   Lens of Sutton

Sufficient land had been obtained near the small village of Kingsley (about three miles south of Bentley) to build an intermediate station and goods yard in an area which the LSWR hoped would produce residential development. As it was, only a modest halt was built and even this was not ready at the time of opening and had to wait until March 7th 1906 before it finally came into use. In their March 10th 1906 edition, the *Farnham Herald* once more briefly covered the opening with the following very short paragraph:-

In connection with the Bentley and Bordon Light Railway, the L & SW Railway Co. have decided to open a halt at Kingsley.

To work the line the LSWR had reached an agreement with the War Department whereby the LSWR would manage, work and maintain the railway, and provide locomotive power, rolling stock and plant of every description suitable and sufficient for the effectual working of the traffic of the railway.

In 1905 the War Department decided to build a standard gauge military-only line from Longmoor to Bordon so that it would connect with the LSWR's light railway at Bordon by way of an exchange siding. The main function for this military line was for training soldiers in railway operation and from 1906 until 1935 was known as the Woolmer Instructional Military Railway but from 1935 onwards the line became known as the Longmoor Military Railway.

A 3¹/₂ mile extension southwards from the military line at Longmoor to Liss on the main Waterloo-Portsmouth line was begun in 1924 and completed in 1933, although surprisingly the physical connection to the main line at Liss was not provided until 1942.

Although the light railway from Bentley to Bordon had all the characteristics of a typical country branch line serving the local community, there's no doubt that its main use were the strong military connections at Bordon. This was never more evident than during the two world wars when many a young man had his last glimpse of Hampshire soil from the carriage window as he left Bordon on his way to war.

After the second world war, things slowed down and it came as no great surprise that passenger services were withdrawn on and from September 16th 1957. The line stayed open for goods and military requirements and even the odd enthusiasts 'Special' but, these services ceased on April 4th 1966 when the light railway between Bentley and Bordon closed completely.

A familiar scene at Bordon as troops march from the station.   Lens of Sutton

Description of the Route

Bentley Station came into being during July 1854, two years after the LSWR opened their Farnham-Alton line on July 28th 1852. At first the Farnham-Alton line was only single tracked and stayed so until June 2nd 1901 before it was doubled.

When the Bordon Light Railway was opened, the 'down' platform was extended to form a bay for the new line. This bay was later separated from the main line platform by iron railings which were added, it is believed, by the Southern Railway who inherited the LSWR at the time of grouping.

For many years the station name board at Bentley offered passengers the following advice: 'BENTLEY CHANGE FOR THE BORDON LIGHT RAILWAY' but, by the 1950's just read BENTLEY.

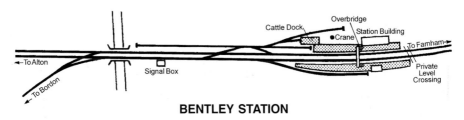

BENTLEY STATION

M7 class 0-4-4T No.30109 in the Bordon bay at Bentley Station on February 2nd 1952.

R.F.Roberts

8

A12 class 0-4-2 No.632 stands at the 'down' platform at Bentley Station bound for Alton, while M7 class 0-4-4T No.28 waits in the Bordon bay during the 1930's. Dr.Ian C.Allen

M7 class 0-4-4T No.30328 waits with pull-and-push set No.32 in the Bordon bay at Bentley Station during the 1950's. The iron railings were thought to have been added by the Southern Railway. R.C.Riley

M7 class 0-4-4T No.30110 waits in the Bordon bay during the 1950's. Lens of Sutton

On leaving the bay, the train for Bordon would use the main 'down' line for 17 chains in the direction of Alton before branching off south. At the junction for Bordon stood the Bentley signal box which was the fourth box in the history of Bentley Station. The first box stood by the entrance to the goods yard and was built when the station opened. This was replaced during the 1880's by a twelve lever box which was situated at the west end of the 'down' platform. When the Farnham-Alton line was doubled on the 2nd June 1901 a third box was built at the east end of the 'down' platform to replace the second one. This third box had a short life as the new line to Bordon required yet another box which was built at the actual junction.

This fourth box was a typical LSWR style signal box built of wood with a hipped slated roof. By the 1950's it contained a 33 lever frame and was equipped with Preece two position instruments for the main line and a Tyer's No.6 tablet instrument for the Bordon line.

The signal box at Bentley near the junction for Bordon on September 26th 1953. Denis Cullum

The junction with the main Farnham-Alton line at Bentley on August 5th 1957. The two tracks soon became a single track leading towards Kingsley Halt (see photograph below). A.E.Bennett

On leaving the main line the single track turned in a southerly direction towards Kingsley Halt and Bordon, climbing a gradient of 1 in 156. After 1 mile 10 chains the line passed over the road at the Blacknest Crossing which in true light railway traditions had no crossing gates and was protected with cattle grids. This level crossing was officially described in the Southern Railway "Particulars of Level Crossings" as Blacknest Road but in fact  it crossed over the road between the small villages of Blacknest and Binsted which today is known as Binsted Road. *The Southern Railway also added an 'a' to the spelling of Binstead.*

The Blacknest Crossing looking back towards Bentley on September 26th 1953.   Denis Cullum

11

From Blacknest Crossing the line gradually dropped towards Kingsley Halt which was 2 miles 57 chains from Bentley. Here the single platform was on the down (east) side of the line and was merely a sleeper faced grass covered earth mound, consisting simply of a nameboard, noticeboard, lamp and a seat. For waiting passengers, not even a shelter was provided.

As previously mentioned, this intermediate halt was opened on March 7th 1906, some months after the line had originally opened. At that time the LSWR had purchased quite an area of land where they had hoped to build a larger station and goods yard to accommodate the residential development that they had expected.

On leaving Kingsley Halt the line crossed on the level the adjoining road which like the Blacknest Crossing was protected by cattle grids. The Southern Railway described this crossing as Binstead Road (again spelt with an 'a') when in fact it was and still is Sickles Lane which leads from the village of Kingsley towards Binsted.

Ungated Level Crossing

To Bentley ⟶

◄— To Bordon

KINGSLEY HALT

The picturesque view at Kingsley Halt, looking towards Bentley on September 14th 1957.
R.F.Roberts

Looking towards Kingsley Halt from about mid-way between Kingsley Halt and Bordon on September 26th 1953.
Denis Cullum

From here the line continued its gradual descent and passed over several bridges of which one crossed over the Kingsley-East Worldham Road before a climb of 1 in 358 and then a descent of 1 in 145 was experienced. Continuing on the level the line then took a very gentle climb towards Bordon. On approaching Bordon Station, the line crossed over a level crossing which the Southern Railway called Whitehill Road when it was and still is Gibbs Lane which leads to Gibbs Farm. Just to add to the confusion, this crossing was also locally known as Marsh's Crossing and also went over the adjoining Longmoor Military Railway which paralleled the Bordon line at this point and, like the other level crossings on the line was protected by cattle grids.

Bordon Station was 4 miles 58 chains from Bentley and was, at first, a two-platformed terminus with a goods shed and yard. The station building was to remain almost unaltered from the time the LSWR built it in 1905. It was constructed mainly of corrugated iron on steel framing and stood on a short brick wall. Because of extra traffic during the first world war, the building was slightly extended in 1916 and a larger wooden canopy was also added to the platform side of the building.

By the 1930's the 'up' platform was rarely used and became very overgrown. Later it was cut back to just over half its original length. It remained rarely used and by the late 1950's was still very much overgrown. The station layout was completed by a signal box and an engine shed. The small wooden ground level signal box was virtually an enlarged ground frame of 20 levers and was situated (as was the engine shed) at the approach to the station on arriving from Kingsley Halt. The engine shed was opened when the line was completed in 1905 and was built of corrugated iron on steel framework for a single road. It was later enlarged and a siding with a coal stage was added but soon after the second world war an engine ran through the back of the shed and from then on the small Bordon engine shed looked a very sorry sight.

When the line was opened, a turntable was also proposed and although a site was prepared a few yards from the signal box, it was never installed.

BORDON STATION

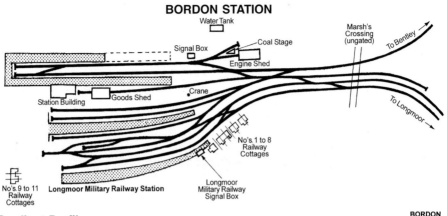

Gradient Profile

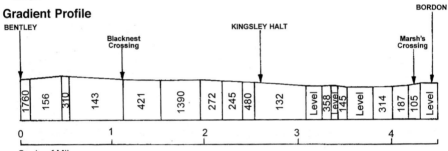

Scale of Miles

The engine shed at Bordon in 1938 before it was damaged by an engine running through the back.

W.A.Camwell

14

Bordon Station on September 26th 1953. Denis Cullum

M7 class 0-4-4T No.30027 stands in front of the derelict engine shed at Bordon while a Railway Enthusiasts Club Special is in the Longmoor Military Railway sidings on September 26th 1953.
Denis Cullum

Water tank, signal box and sorry remains of the engine shed at Bordon on April 12th 1952. Denis Cullum

Motive Power and Rolling Stock

The small engine shed at Bordon was used in the early days for stabling an engine overnight and also for the odd visiting troop engine but, the lines' motive power was provided from the Guildford shed.

It is interesting to note that in the early years of the line, LSWR H13 class Steam Railcars designed by Dugald Drummond (the LSWR Locomotive Superintendent from 1895 to 1912) were used. These Railcars had the engine portion encased in the coachwork unlike Drummond's original design which had both the engine and coach mounted on a single underframe. By 1916 the Railcars were withdrawn and converted to trailer carriages.

From 1916 the line was mainly worked by the LSWR O2 class 0-4-4T's designed by William Adams (the LSWR Locomotive Superintendent from 1878 to 1895) which was the type of locomotive seen on many of the LSWR's branch lines at the time.

Also making an appearance at about this time was LSWR Adams T1 class 0-4-4T's plus the class of locomotive to dominate the passenger service in later years, the LSWR Drummond M7 class 0-4-4T's.

For the increased Great War traffic, a LSWR 302 class Goods 0-6-0 engine designed by W.G.Beattie (the LSWR Locomotive Superintendent from 1871 to 1878) and a LSWR Adams 415 class 4-4-2T engine were introduced.

During the 1930's the former London Brighton & South Coast Railway D1 class 0-4-2T's designed by William Stroudley which were based at Guildford at the time were used on the line.

After World War II the passenger services were worked almost exclusively by Drummond M7 class 0-4-4T's right up until the passenger services were withdrawn in 1957.

H13 class Steam Railcar No.10 in the bay at Bentley Station c.1910.   John Gough Collection

O2 class 0-4-4T No.204 which worked the line in the early 1920's. W.L.Kenning/Adrian Vaughan Collection

T1 class 0-4-4T No.10 at Bordon Station during the early 1920's. W.L.Kenning/Adrian Vaughan Collection

Goods trains were usually worked from Farnham either by Bulleid Q1 class 0-6-0's or Maunsell N and U class 2-6-0's. Sometimes by Drummond 700 class 0-6-0's. Former South Eastern & Chatham Railway C class 0-6-0's designed by H.S.Wainwright were also known to have occasionally worked the goods service which was handled in the final years by diesel electric locomotives.

To work the special troop trains over the line, Drummond's 4-4-0's T9s, L12s and S11s were all put to full use with War Department (later Army Dept.) locomotives taking over at Bordon exchange sidings for work over the Longmoor Military Railway.

Apart from the Steam Railcars, passengers in the early years were mainly carried in LSWR gated stock, followed later by compartment pull-and-push two carriage sets.

From 1949 onwards, the passenger service consisted mainly of 'Ironclad' corridor sets made up of ex-LSWR and ex-South Eastern & Chatham Railway paired stock.

Military specials over the line used a whole variety of stock including 'Netley' ambulance vans which were seen from time to time.

M7 class 0-4-4T No.30109 at Bordon Station on April 12th 1952.   R.F.Roberts

415 class 4-4-2T No.428 at Bordon. This locomotive was used on the line during the Great War.
W.L.Kenning/Adrian Vaughan Collection

D1 class 0-4-2T No.2260 heads the Bordon train having just left the main line in the 1930's. Dr.Ian C.Allen

C class 0-6-0 No.1294 passing over Sickles Lane at Kingsley Halt with a goods train for Bordon in the early 1950's. E.C.Griffiths

Pull-and-push 'Ironclad' set No.384 at Bordon Station on April 7th 1951. G.W.Puntis

M7 class 0-4-4T No.30328 leaving Kingsley Halt for Bordon with a pull-and-push two carriage set on September 4th 1954.   Tony Wright

Diesel electric locomotive No.D6545 approaching Bordon with a goods train on March 28th 1966. At this time the Longmoor Military Railway signal arms had been removed while the exchange siding was cut back and no longer crossed the road. The Longmoor Military Railway can be seen leading off to the right of the photograph.   Tony Wright

Operation

The signalling for trains arriving at Bentley from Bordon was so arranged that they terminated at the 'up' platform and then had to shunt back on to the 'down' line to gain access to the Bordon bay. Trains from Bordon were therefore timed to arrive when neither an 'up' nor a 'down' train on the main line was due.

Although fitted with the Tyers No.6 electric tablet system, the line was unusual in that at various times the one engine in steam principle was also adopted. During the mid 1920's, traffic at Bordon had fallen off to such an extent that it was decided that requirements could easily be met by utilising the one engine in steam principle which meant disconnecting (although retaining) the tablet instruments at Bentley and Bordon signal boxes. By November 1927 the signal box at Bordon was reduced to the status of a ground frame. During peak periods, namely troop movements, the tablet instruments were reconnected and brought back into use, so that the line could link up with the Longmoor Military Railway who had their own signal box in their sidings at Bordon. Later the one engine in steam principle was abolished and by the early 1950's the line had returned to the tablet system.

BENTLEY JUNCTION AND BORDON.

To be carried out on Sunday, 20th November.

After 12.5 a.m. on Sunday, 20th November the tablet instruments in Bentley Junction and Bordon signal boxes will be disconnected and put out of use and the line between these points worked in accordance with the Regulations for working Single Lines of Railway by only one engine in steam or two or more engines coupled together as shown on page 53 of the Western Section Appendix, an ordinary train staff being provided.

The signal box at Bordon will be worked as a ground frame and be released by a key on the Train Staff. The road will be normally set from the single line to No. 1 platform road.

A yellow location light on a post, 12 feet in height, will be provided on the down side of the line, 640 yards from Bordon signal box, to enable Enginemen to readily locate their position when approaching the station.

The undermentioned signal arms at Bordon will be removed from the posts :—

To Nos. 1 and 2 and dock roads homes.

From Nos. 1 and 2 and dock roads starting.

The work will be in progress from 12.5 a.m. Mr. Evemy to provide flagman, as required. (R.16,888.)

Signal instructions No.33 (1927), dated November 15th 1927.

M7 class 0-4-4T No.30027 shunting a single carriage into the bay at Bentley Station to form a special three carriage train for Bordon on September 26th 1953. Denis Cullum

Handing over the tablet for Bordon at the Bentley signal box during the 1950's. E.C.Griffiths

Life on the "Bordon Light"

When the line was opened in 1905, the LSWR built eleven cottages at Bordon Station for the staff employed to work on the line. No's. 1 to 4 were two pairs of semi-detached dwellings and No's. 5 to 7 made up a short terrace. No.8 was the stationmaster's detached house. No's. 9 to 11 were built at the other end of the station and were also a short terrace.

Mr. Langridge, who had the honour of driving the first train over the line, lived at No.3 and Mr. Waterman who was also one of the original drivers lived at No.7. One of the first guards on the line, Mr. Ernest Siggery, lived at No.10. Other employees living in the cottages during those early days were Messrs.Chandler, Knight, Petherbridge, Chant, Norman, Winter and Peters.

One of the Bordon stationmasters was a Mr. Thatcher. Another employee, Mr. Pretty, lived at Kingsley while Mr. Bone and Mr. Yeomans lived near Oakhanger.

One of the first guards to work on the line was Ernest Siggery who lived at No.10. Mrs.W.H.Roberts Collection

Looking across the Longmoor Military Railway at Bordon towards No's. 1 to 8 station cottages which can be seen behind the Longmoor Military Railway signal box. Lens of Sutton

Railway staff at Bordon Station c. 1910. Lens of Sutton

Timetables

APRIL 1910

	a.m.	a.m.	a.m.	a.m.	p.m.	p.m.	p.m.	p.m.	p.m.	p.m.	p.m.	p.m.	p.m.	p.m.	SUNDAYS a.m.	p.m.	p.m.	p.m.	p.m.
Bentley	7.44	8.40	10.53	11.46	b1.22	2.55	3.50	4.52	5.44	6.50	7.14	9.03	9.43	12.03	8.50	11.03	4.50	8.08	11.49
Kingsley Halt	7.51	8.47	11.00	11.53	b1.29	3.02	3.57	4.59	5.51	6.57	7.21	9.10	9.50	12.10	8.58	11.10	4.57	8.15	11.56
Bordon	7.57	8.53	11.06	11.59	b1.35	3.08	4.03	5.05	5.57	7.03	7.26	9.16	9.56	12.16	9.03	11.16	5.03	8.21	12.02

	a.m.	a.m.	a.m.	a.m.	p.m.	p.m.	p.m.	p.m.	p.m.	p.m.	p.m.	p.m.	p.m.	p.m.	SUNDAYS a.m.	a.m.	p.m.	p.m.
Bordon	7.08	8.12	9.20	11.17	12.52	1.15	2.15	3.17	4.10	5.10	6.20	7.37	8.35	9.18	11.00	8.20	10.30	4.24	7.36
Kingsley Halt	7.17	8.18	9.27	11.24	12.59	1.22	2.22	3.24	4.17	5.17	6.27	7.44	8.42	9.25	11.07	8.27	10.37	4.31	7.43
Bentley	7.22	8.26	9.34	11.31	1.06	1.29	2.29	3.31	4.24	5.24	6.34	7.50	8.49	9.32	11.14	8.34	10.44	4.38	7.50

b 8 minutes later on Saturdays

JULY 1938

	a.m.	a.m.	a.m.	p.m.	p.m.	p.m.	p.m.	p.m.	p.m.	p.m.	p.m.	p.m.	p.m.	SUNDAYS a.m.	a.m.	p.m.	p.m.	p.m.	p.m.
Bentley	8.15	9.15	10.15	12.45	1.45	3.45	4.45	5.45	6.45	7.45	8.45	9.45	11.15	8.45	9.45	3.45	6.45	9.50	12.23
Kingsley Halt	8.23	9.23	10.23	12.53	1.53	3.53	4.53	5.53	6.53	7.53	8.53	9.53	11.23	......	......	......	......	......	
Bordon	8.30	9.30	10.30	1.00	2.00	4.00	5.00	6.00	7.00	8.00	9.00	10.00	11.30	8.59	9.59	3.59	6.59	10.04	12.37

	a.m.	a.m.	a.m.	p.m.	p.m.	p.m.	p.m.	p.m.	p.m.	p.m.	p.m.	p.m.	S.O. p.m.	SUNDAYS a.m.	a.m.	p.m	p.m	p.m
Bordon	7.40	8.40	9.40	12.10	1.10	3.10	4.10	5.10	6.10	7.10	8.10	9.10	10.10	9.10	10.10	4.10	7.10	10.10
Kingsley Halt	7.46	8.46	9.46	12.16	1.16	3.16	4.16	5.16	6.16	7.16	8.16	9.16	10.16	......	......	......	......	
Bentley	7.55	8.55	9.55	12.25	1.25	3.25	4.25	5.25	6.25	7.25	8.25	9.25	10.25	9.24	10.24	4.24	7.24	10.24

S.O. Saturdays Only

Tickets

Tickets from the G.R.Croughton Collection

Closure to Passengers

After World War II, the Bordon Light Railway continued its leisurely existence with a M7 0-4-4T and a pull-and-push two carriage set rattling to and fro between Bentley and Bordon.

Apart from the occasional troop special bound for the Longmoor Military Railway the line was now becoming a financial liability and so it was no great surprise when in the changing world of the 1950's that 'Withdrawal of Passenger Train Services' notices appeared advising that the passenger train service would be withdrawn on and from September 16th 1957.

(*Above left*) The 'Withdrawal of Passenger Train Service' notice at Bordon Station.　R.N.Thornton
(*Above right*) M7 class 0-4-4T No.30027 approaching Bordon with a troop special on September 26th 1953.　S.C.Nash

M7 class 0-4-4T No.30110 with a pull-and-push set approaching Kingsley Halt on the last day of passenger service on September 15th 1957.　R.N.Thornton

Although passenger trains were withdrawn on and from September 16th 1957 the line remained open for goods and also to meet military requirements. It would probably have closed completely if the Longmoor Military Railway could have been served from Liss, but the frequency of electric trains on the Waterloo-Portsmouth line made the exchange of heavy traffic quite difficult.

An interesting excursion was organised by the Railway Correspondence and Travel Society on the October 4th 1958 when a special train ran from Waterloo to the Longmoor Military Railway via Liss and then back to Waterloo via the light railway from Bordon. Pulling this special train over the Longmoor Military Railway was Army Department locomotive 2-8-0 No.400 'Sir Guy Williams'. From the sidings at Bordon, former LSWR Drummond T9 4-4-0 No.30120, which had hauled the special from Waterloo to Liss and then ran light from Liss to Bordon took over once more and pulled from Bordon back to Waterloo via Bentley.

Another interesting visit was made on the January 9th 1966 when the Locomotive Club of Great Britain organised a special train from Waterloo to Eastleigh employing the last Maunsell S15 class 4-6-0 in working order, No.30837. On the outward journey, this special train worked via Alton and on reaching Bentley it deviated to Bordon and back with Maunsell U class 2-6-0 No.31639 in charge. This special visit was also repeated on January 16th 1966.

T9 class 4-4-0 No.30120 with the Railway Correspondence and Travel Society special train in the Longmoor Military Railway sidings at Bordon on October 4th 1958.　　　　　　R.C.Riley

U class 2-6-0 No.31639 with the Locomotive Club of Great Britain special train approaching the Blacknest Crossing on January 16th 1966.　　　　　　Mrs.J.M.Munday Collection

Diesel electric locomotive No.D6545 prepares to run round a goods train at Bordon Station on March 28th 1966.   Tony Wright

No.D6545 running round the goods train at Bordon Station.   Tony Wright

With work completed at Bordon, No.D6545 heads back to the main line at Bentley after passing Kingsley Halt.   Tony Wright

Despite the frequency of electric trains on the Waterloo-Portsmouth line at Liss, a decision was taken later to abandon the Bentley to Bordon railway and so, on April 4th 1966, the line was closed completely.

Although the line had officially closed, the Railway Correspondence and Travel Society ran another special train on Saturday April 16th 1966 from Waterloo via Woking to Liss, then over the Longmoor Military Railway to Bordon. From Bordon over the light railway to Bentley, then back to Waterloo via Farnham, Ascot, Staines, Windsor, Hounslow and Barnes. Pulling this special train over the Longmoor Military Railway and between Bordon and Bentley was Army Department locomotive 2-10-0 No. 600 'Gordon' which has become immortalised as 'Gordon the Blue Engine' in the Reverend W.Awdry's famous 'Thomas the Tank Engine' stories.

A repeat performance of this tour was once more carried out by the Railway Correspondence and Travel Society on Saturday April 30th 1966.

Track lifting started between Bordon and Bentley in November 1966 and was soon completed.

The Longmoor Military Railway was not to last much longer than the Bordon Light Railway and was closed on October 31st 1969.

The demolition train shunting on the main 'down' line before going on the Bordon line for track lifting on November 17th 1966.
Jim Bodkin

Blacknest Crossing just before the track was lifted on November 17th 1966. Jim Bodkin

Kingsley Halt after track lifting on November 17th 1966. Jim Bodkin

The Present Scene

Like so many similar light railways and branch lines which were closed in the 1950's and 1960's, very little evidence remains of the Bordon Light Railway to remind us what the line was really like.

At Bentley Station, the bay for Bordon is still there but looks very forlorn and deserted as it lies trackless, backed by a grassy bank and trees.

The signal box which once stood at the junction for Bordon has now been moved for preservation to the Mid-Hants 'Watercress Line' Railway and the spot where the line branched off from the main Alton line is now very overgrown.

Heading south, the remains of the line are very hard to detect and seem to have been reclaimed by the lush, green, rolling countryside although the rough alignment can be picked up on the approach to Blacknest Crossing.

From Blacknest Crossing, the trackbed can easily be spotted as it now forms a farm track but, towards the former halt at Kingsley it completely disappears.

At the site of Kingsley Halt one would never know that the small platform ever existed although the slight mound in the field plus one solitary poplar tree (at the time of writing) does give some indication.

The former level crossing over the adjoining Sickles Lane is well hidden with brambles on both sides of the road and although the overgrown trackbed heading towards Bordon can be seen, it soon disappears.

The bridge which crossed over the Kingsley-East Worldham Road has now been removed and from here to Bordon only the odd trace can be found.

The whole area which was Bordon Station and the sidings for the Longmoor Military Railway has been built over and is now a trading estate. Only the name Old Station Way and the cottages built by the LSWR for their employees give any indication that this ever was a railway station.

The former Bordon bay at Bentley Station. April 6th 2009.   Author

Conclusion

With passenger traffic dropping away and road transport taking on much more of the military work, it was therefore not surprising that the Bordon Light Railway was considered to have fulfilled its useful role.

From when the line was opened in 1905 until it closed, first for passengers in 1957 and then for goods in 1966, there's no doubt that it was of great value to the Army Camp at Bordon and the local community in general. It also of course, provided another important link by connecting the Longmoor Military Railway with the outside world via the junction at Bentley but, when this service was switched to the junction at Liss, the fate of the Bordon Light Railway was finally sealed.

Now both the Bordon Light Railway and the Longmoor Military Railway have passed into history and are just memories of times gone by, but, times which in one way or another were very important in this country.

M7 class 0-4-4T No.30110 at Kingsley Halt with a pull-and-push two carriage set on September 7th 1957.
Tony Wright

C class 0-6-0 No.1294 with a goods train near Kingsley Halt in the early 1950's. E.C.Griffiths

The Future

Since writing and publishing the first edition of this booklet in 1987, Bordon and Whitehill have grown to such an extent that there has even been talk of reinstating the line (or a line) from Bentley to Bordon. East Hampshire District Council have led a successful bid to transform Bordon and Whitehill into an Eco-town and as part of this it wants to reduce the number of car journeys residents need to make.

The late Peter Gauld said in November 2006 while he was chairman of the Bordon and Whitehill Transport Group, leading the bid for a railway connection, "If and when the venture starts to take off, it will need all the public support it can get as it is realised that progress through procedures will be slow and costly, but essential for future generations to come".

Whether the railway is reinstated or not, it does leave some hope that trains to Bordon may not after all have finally passed into history.

Acknowledgements

My sincere thanks to all the photographers who kindly supplied photographs for the first edition of this publication in 1987 and also this revised edition. Thanks also to the Farnham Herald and the Farnham Museum for their help. As always, my thanks to Norman Branch for reading my text and to James Christian and Dan Perkins of Binfield Print & Design for their help.

The former platform at Bordon Station on July 4th 1971. The railway cottages and the disused signal box of the Longmoor Military Railway can be seen on the right of the photograph. E.Course

Looking towards the former buffer stops at Bordon Station in June 1968. Nick Catford